YOUNG ARCHITECT

Animal Homes

by Saranne Taylor

Illustrated by Moreno Chiacchiera and Michelle Todd

Crabtree Publishing Company

Crabtree Publishing Company
www.crabtreebooks.com
1-800-387-7650

Published in Canada
616 Welland Ave.
St. Catharines, ON
L2M 5V6

Published in the United States
PMB 59051, 350 Fifth Ave.
59th Floor,
New York, NY

Author: Saranne Taylor
Illustrators: Moreno Chiacchiera, Michelle Todd
Project coordinator: Kelly McNiven
Editor: Shirley Duke
Proofreader: Crystal Sikkens
**Production coordinator
        and prepress technician:** Ken Wright
Print coordinator: Katherine Berti

Photographs:
Pg 4 – stoonn
Pg 7 – (tl) Lisa Strachan (tr) Kitch Bain (b) Linda & Kevan
            Sunderland, Sunderland Wildlife Photography
Pg 14 – (l) Ivan Kuzmin (r) Ficmajstr
Pg 15 – (tl) Jiri Haureljuk (tr) fotandy (b) Mopic
Pg 16 – (t) wonderisland (m) khazari (b) Joseph Calev
Pg 18 - Simon Greig
Pg 19 – Valery Shanin
Pg 20 – Henk Bentlage
Pg 22 - (l) JIANG HONGYAN (r) Robert Eastman
Pg 23 – (tl) Pan Xunbin (tm) Robert Eastman
            (tr) Jiang Zhongyan
Pg 24 – Ideas_supermarket
Pg 26 – PHOTO FUN
Pg 27- S-F
Pg 28 - diepre

All images are Shutterstock.com unless otherwise stated.

Every attempt has been made to clear copyright. Should there
be any inadvertent omissions, please notify the publisher.

Printed in Hong Kong/082014/BK20140613

Library and Archives Canada Cataloguing in Publication

Taylor, Saranne, author
        Animal homes / Saranne Taylor ; illustrated by Moreno
Chiacchiera and Michelle Todd.

(Young architect)
Includes index.
Issued in print and electronic formats.
ISBN 978-0-7787-1438-5 (bound).--ISBN 978-0-7787-1454-5 (pbk.)
ISBN 978-1-4271-1577-5 (pdf).--ISBN 978-1-4271-1573-7 (html)

        1. Animals--Habitations--Juvenile literature. I. Chiacchiera, Moreno,
illustrator II. Todd, Michelle, 1978-, illustrator III. Title.

QL756.T396 2014   j591.56'4   C2014-903588-8
                                              C2014-903589-6

Library of Congress Cataloging-in-Publication Data

Taylor, Saranne, author.
 Animal homes / by Saranne Taylor ; illustrated by Moreno Chiacchiera and Michelle
Todd.
      pages cm. -- (Young architect)
 Includes index.
  ISBN 978-0-7787-1438-5 (reinforced library binding) -- ISBN 978-0-7787-1454-5 (pbk.) --
ISBN 978-1-4271-1577-5 (electronic pdf) -- ISBN 978-1-4271-1573-7 (electronic html)
1. Animals--Habitations--Juvenile literature. 2. Animal behavior--Juvenile literature. [1.
Animals--Habits and behavior.] I. Chiacchiera, Moreno, illustrator. II. Todd, Michelle,
1978- illustrator. III. Title. IV. Series: Young architect.

QL756.T396 2015
591.56'4--dc23
                                              2014020112

Contents

Introduction

Animals are surprisingly amazing architects and **engineers**. They are able to create complicated designs and can even use their own bodies as building tools! Some of them work alone to create their homes. Others work in groups—sometimes with thousands of members! Every one has a particular job to do. Not only that, but the way they build their homes has inspired many architects and their designs.

4

Weaver birds

Weaver birds are found in Africa and Asia. They get their name from the skillful way the males weave their nests.

Each **species**, or type, uses different materials to weave their nests into all kinds of sizes and shapes. They use things such as twigs, grass, and leaves, which they tear into strips. Then the males weave them together using their feet and beaks.

Some weaver birds build individual nests, but most live in big groups called **colonies**. They make large nests with different rooms known as chambers—like an apartment building for birds! These shared homes can house over 100 pairs of birds.

Tie a piece of grass around a twig. This forms the base of the nest.

Weave a circular shape by tying more strips of grass together. Then do the same to form the roof.

Build a tube at the bottom to make a private entrance to the nest.

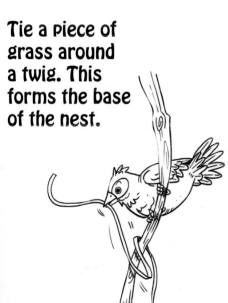

Location and design

Animals choose a place for their homes and create a design based on their special needs.

Weaver birds often build their colonies near water so that animals cannot attack them. Their nests are usually round with a small narrow entrance at the bottom. This keeps other birds or snakes from stealing their eggs or young, and also prevents water from entering their home in the rainy season.
They even choose to live in trees which are full of thorns or insects that bite to scare off **predators**.

All species of animal are born with special skills which help them build their homes. This is called **instinct**. It is an incredible part of nature which scientists cannot fully explain.

- Architect's words -
Choosing a site
Just like birds and other animals, humans decide on a **site** that meets their needs. Those who want a home near work or school, or near a bus or train station so they can use public transit, would probably choose a site in the city. Others who want to grow their own crops or raise animals would pick a site in the countryside.

6

Animal tools

How can animals build their homes without tools? Surprisingly, lots of animals have special parts of their body, which they use to help them.

The chimpanzee, like many members of the ape family, is able to use its fingers to move and shape sticks into a nest.

The puffin has a strong beak that looks like a cone. This shape helps with tearing and weaving the leaves.

The female alligator is an expert nest builder. She uses her jaws to gather and drag vegetation to the chosen spot. She uses her body and tail to clear the area and digs a hole for her eggs with her hind legs.

The magpie's nest

Long ago, the only bird who knew how to build a nest was the magpie. She was the best builder of all, so the other birds asked her to show them how it was done.

They all gathered around and she started to teach them. The trouble was, they weren't very patient listeners ...

The magpie
began by
taking some
mud and
making
a sort of
round shape.

That was enough for the thrush,
who flew off to build its nest
just like that.

Next, the magpie found some twigs and placed them around the mud shape. Right away, the blackbird disappeared thinking it knew everything about strong nests. But the magpie hadn't finished and continued to build ...

She went on by packing some more mud over the twigs. "What a good idea," said the owl, and it left at once to start work on its own home.

But still the magpie had more to do. She used extra twigs to weave around the outside and feathers to line and soften the inside.

All the birds watched the magpie build part of the nest, but none of them waited until the end of the lesson.

That is why all birds' nests are built in different ways.

The beaver's lodge

Beavers are found in forest areas in North America, Asia, and Europe. They are extraordinary engineers. Not only do they create clever designs, but they build an amazing home for a whole community.

Beavers are a type of rodent. Rodents are animals that have large gnawing teeth. They are **nocturnal**, which means they are most active at night.

They build their homes in rivers and streams next to forests. They can live in the water as well as on land. This is because they have waterproof fur, webbed back feet, and special eyelids that act a bit like goggles! They also have a large, flat tail which they use like a rudder to turn and steady themselves when they are swimming or diving.

Their front feet are used like hands to carry building materials and to construct homes that are quite complex.

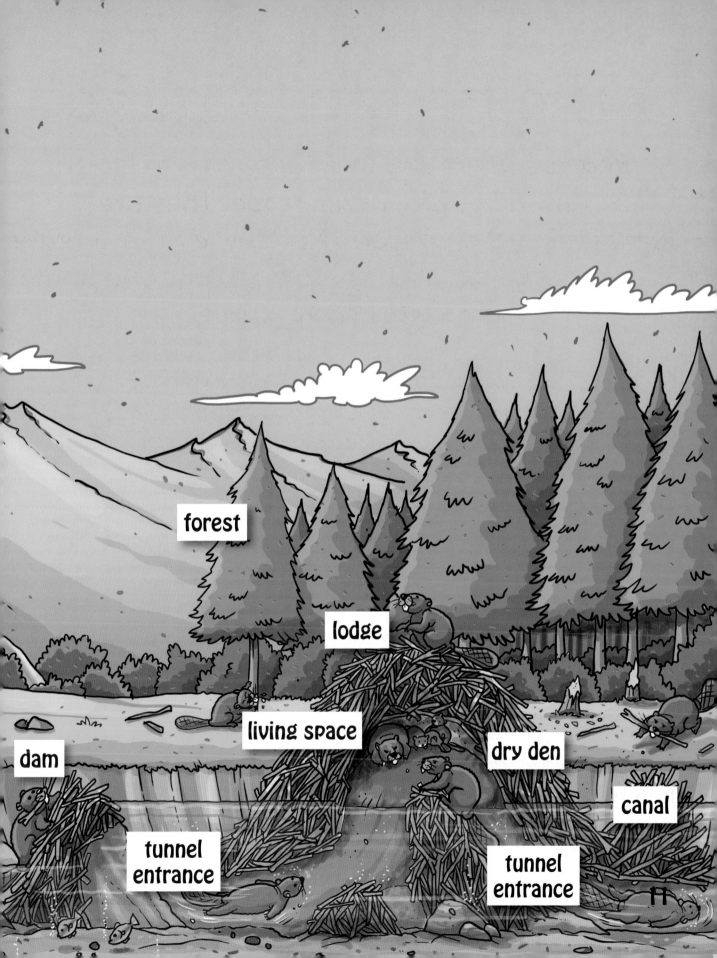

Structure and ...

Beavers build three sections to their homes: one or two dams, a set of **canals**, and the lodge.

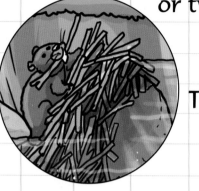
building the dam

Dam

The dam holds back the water of the river and forms a deep pond. Here, they are protected from their predators, who can't reach their homes.

the lodge home

Canal

They also build several canals to form a kind of transport system. They float food and building materials along these canals because it is easier to move heavy things in water.

in a tunnel entrance

Lodge

The lodge where they live is a dome-shaped structure. It has several different spaces: an area to dry off, a nesting chamber, a dry den where the family lives and eats, a food storage area, two tunnel entrances, and a tube for fresh air.

... construction

Using powerful front teeth, they gnaw their way through a tall tree near a river or stream.

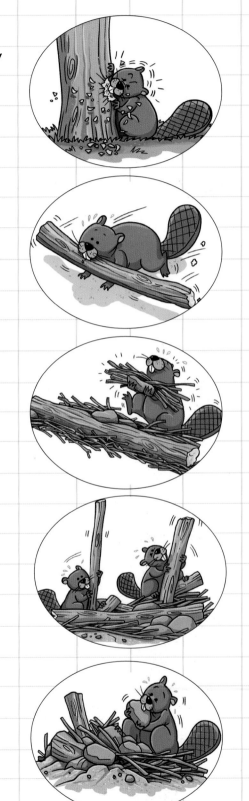

Once it falls, they pull it across the water to create the base of the dam.

They then pile sticks, stones, and mud on top until the dam is above the water level and can stop the flow of the river.

The lodges can be ten feet (three meters) tall! The beavers use wood they have cut down to place several poles upright in the water.

Then, they join these poles together with branches placed across them.

Any holes in these walls are filled with mud and weeds until no water can get through.

What is a colony?

Weaver birds and beavers have one thing in common—they join others from their species to live together in colonies.

A colony is a group of animals, all of the same kind, that live together in a community. Animals live in colonies to better protect themselves against predators. In a colony everyone contributes and helps. They work as a team, and if they have to build a new home, each member of the colony has a special job to do.

Bats live in colonies, which can have more than one million members.

A colony of frogs is also called an army!

Here are some more examples of animal colonies ...

Seals have flippers in place of feet, which makes them better at swimming than moving on land.

A mischief is another name for a colony of mice.

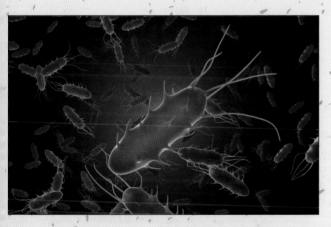

Bacteria are one-celled life-forms that are so small you have to look at them through a microscope. Their colonies grow so fast, they are almost impossible to count.

- Architect's notes -
A building team

Just like in a colony, when we want to build a new home we use a team of workers who have specific jobs to do:

Architect - designs the building
Surveyor - measures property and locates the boundaries
Contractor - manages all the work
Bricklayer - builds walls with different building blocks
Carpenter - does the woodworking
Plumber - connects the pipes to move water
Electrician - wires the building for electricity to light and run the building

The termite colony

One amazing colony builder is the termite - a tiny, wood-eating insect that looks a little like an ant. It creates a tall structure made of mud, soil, wood, and saliva.

Members of the community are divided into groups called **castes**, and each caste has a special job to do within the colony.

The queen lays the eggs—sometimes more than 20,000 in one day! She is much larger than the rest of the termites.

queen

The soldier termites protect the nest. They have large jaws to use as weapons against predators.

soldier

The workers find and store food while looking after the young. They make up the largest group in the colony and are also the builders and caretakers of the structure.

worker

Termite colonies are a well-organized community. They need to be organized with millions of occupants!

They all live inside a huge network of tunnels. These tunnels include spaces to grow and store food, a nursery for new eggs and growing young, and a water source in the cellar, which also helps keep the inside cool.

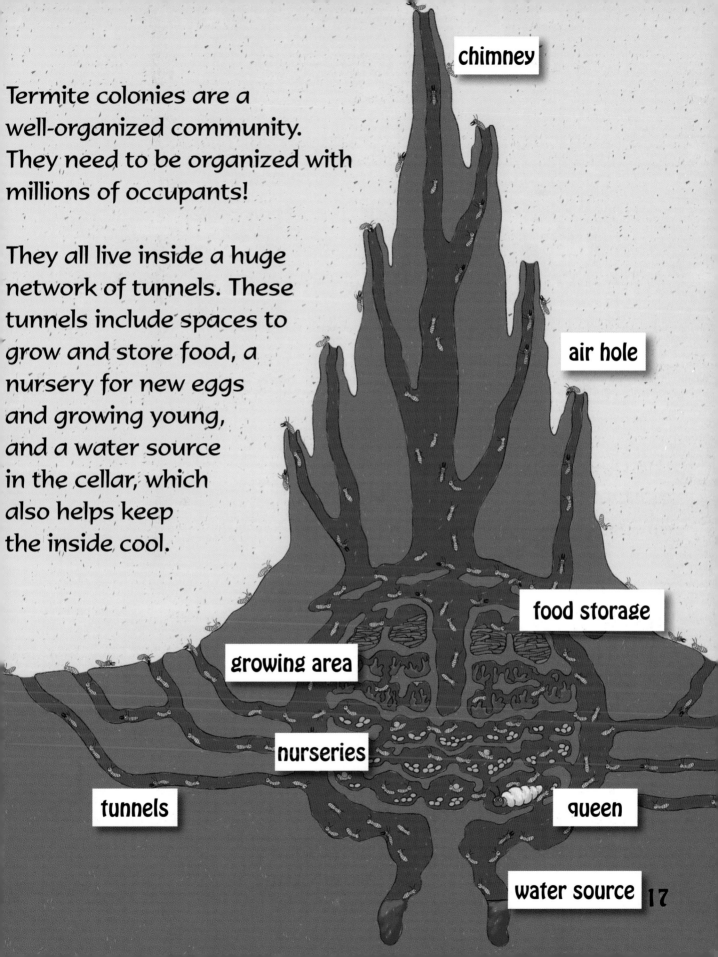

chimney

air hole

food storage

growing area

nurseries

tunnels

queen

water source

17

Architect's notebook
Air flow chimneys

Termite mounds have a special design that controls the temperature inside their home! This idea is so smart that architects have used it in their own plans for buildings around the world.

Termites hate to be hot! One species called the compass termite builds a tall, thin mound so the mound never gets too much sun on its surface.

Termites also use air conditioning. They create a chimney through the center of the mound and make lots of holes all over the structure.

Then, by opening and closing the holes during the day, they are able to let warm air out of the top and bring cool air in at the base.

warm air

cool air

Termite mounds can be as high as ten feet (three meters)!

18

Many of the air conditioning systems that pump cool air into our modern buildings are powered by electricity. This uses a great deal of fuel, which is harmful to the environment.

But we don't need to use electric energy—there are other ways to keep a building cool ...

Wind catchers in Yazd, Iran

These open towers are on the roof of an old house in Iran, where it is very hot all year round. They are special chimneys which catch the cool wind and drag it down into the home below. This controls the temperature inside, just like in the termite mound. It keeps the people who live and work there more comfortable.

Burrowers

Another way to keep cool is to dig a burrow. One of the most amazing burrowing animals is the prairie dog. These animals need underground homes because they live in a part of North America that gets very hot in the summer and very cold in the winter. Their burrows provide them with protection against harsh weather and predators.

Prairie dog burrows are made up of tunnels that can be up to 33 feet (10 meters) long and 10 feet (3 meters) deep.

The tunnels are connected by chambers.

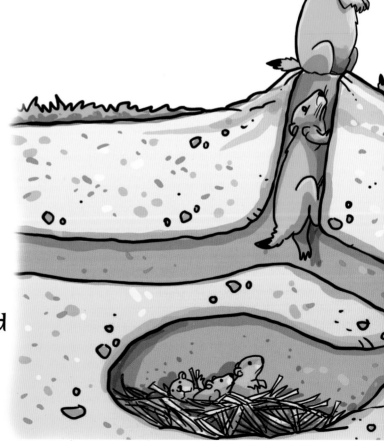

Each of the chambers has a different use. There are areas used only at night or in the winter, and shallow chambers to hide from enemies.

Nursery chambers are dug in the deepest parts of the burrow to protect the young.

Upper chambers are created to avoid flooding.

There are usually about six entrance holes to the burrow, spread over a wide area.

Some of the holes have mounds built around them. This stops water from entering the home. It also gives the prairie dogs a better view of predators that might be planning an attack!

Digging down

Many animals dig underground homes to keep safe from predators and to stay cool and dry.

Rabbits live in colonies and dig a very large system of burrows called a **warren**. They usually build on sloping hills to keep water from entering their homes.

Earthworms spend their whole life underground. They dig through the earth by using the muscles and **bristles** along their body to move them forward.

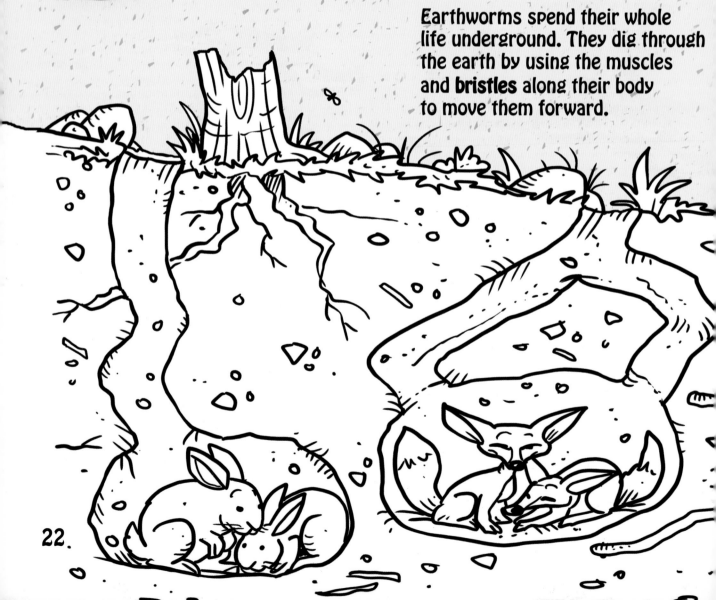

Armadillos are shy animals found mostly in South America. They use their large claws to tunnel out their dens. Their dens are usually a single underground passage a little wider than their body.

The fennec fox lives in the desert and digs its den in the sand. It sometimes connects its den with other families so they can live together.

Clams are animals that burrow into the sand or mud under the sea. They have two shells and a soft body. Part of their body is called a foot, which they use to burrow into the sea bed.

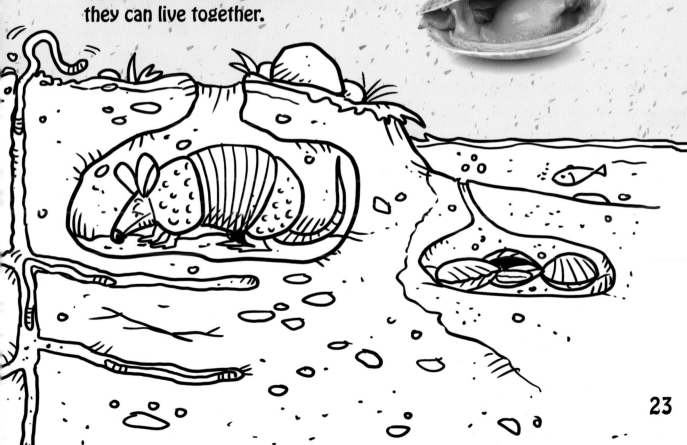

Bees and wasps

Bees and wasps come from the same group of insects. They both build nests as a home for their colony.

Some bees' nests are found in caves and hollow trees, while others hang from trees or buildings.

Bees have special body parts called glands. These glands make a wax that they use to create a **honeycomb**. Honeycombs are made up of hundreds of units called cells, which are placed side by side and back to back.

The cells in the center of the honeycomb hold the eggs and young bees. The outer cells are used to store food.

Female worker bees build the honeycomb.

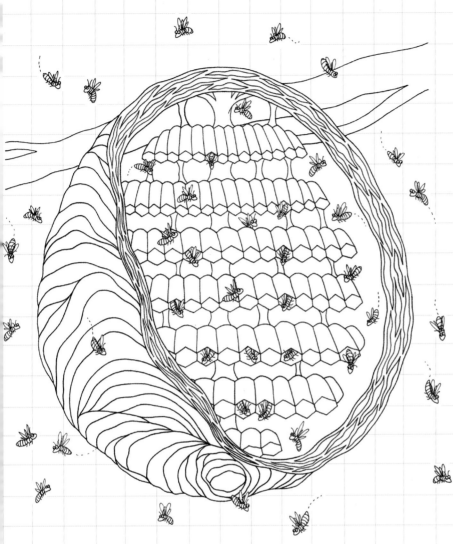

Some wasps use mud to build their homes. Most chew up wood to form a pulp. They use the pulp to create papery nests that they attach to the side of a wall or a branch of a tree.

Hexagons

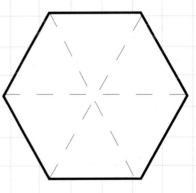

The cells in both bee and wasp nests are the same shape. They are all **hexagons.**

A hexagon is a six-sided shape that is seen a lot in nature, from snowflakes to turtle shells. This formation creates a strong structure because it is made of triangles that fit together tightly.

25

Spiders

A spider creates its home by weaving a web. It is an **arthropod**, which is an animal with bendable legs and a skeleton on the outside.

A spider web is made of sticky silk. A spider makes the silk using special parts at the back of its body called **spinnerets**. First, the spider makes straight lines of silk that meet in the middle. Then it creates the spiral shape by circling over the straight lines, starting from the outside and slowly moving to the center.

Spirals

The most common type of spider's web we see is based on a spiral shape.

A spiral is a curved shape that starts from a center point, then moves around in continuing circles.

The Cayan Tower in Dubai Marina looks like a skyscraper that's been twisted.

Wildlife hotel

One of the best ways to see wildlife close-up is to build a wildlife hotel. It can attract important insects and other small animals to your garden.

A wildlife hotel is a structure made from natural materials. It has different sections that attract insects, such as butterflies and bees, and provides them with a place to lay their eggs or look after their young.

Insects are very important to us. They travel from plant to plant carrying **pollen**, which helps produce seeds allowing new plants to grow. This process is called pollination.

Some wildlife will also use the hotel to **hibernate**, which means they go into a deep sleep during the winter months.

A wildlife hotel

28

Build a wildlife hotel!

Choose a spot in the garden. It needs
to be somewhere that provides sun, shade,
and shelter from the rain.

Scraps of materials such as bamboo,
straw, leaves, pieces of wood, grass
stalks, and even old pots, bricks, and
clay are grouped in piles inside.

Straw and leaves
must stay dry
to encourage
insects to burrow
and hibernate.

Bamboo and grass stalks
are great places for laying
eggs, so they must be
on the warm side of
the hotel.

Stones, bricks, and clay are placed near the bottom
where it is cool—a perfect place for frogs and toads
to live and hibernate.

Glossary

arthropod Groups of animals with jointed legs, an outer skeleton, and a segmented body

bristles Short, stiff hairs

canal A waterway built to transport heavy objects

caste A member of a group with a particular job to do.

colony A group of animals from the same species that live together

engineers People that use math, science, and creative thinking to design things and solve problems

hexagon A six-sided shape often found in nature

hibernate To be inactive or in a deep sleep during the winter months

honeycomb The wax structure made by bees to store food and protect their eggs and young

instinct A natural skill that an animal is born with

nocturnal Animals that are active at night rather than during the daytime

pollen The tiny dust-like particles on flowers that bees spread to other flowers

predator An animal that hunts other others for food

rodent An animal with large gnawing teeth

site A place or location where a building will be built

species A group of similar living things that can make babies with one another

spinneret The part of a spider which makes the silk thread used for its web

spire A tall, narrow structure that comes to a point, often built on the top of a tower

warren A large underground home built by rabbits with connecting burrows

Learning more

Books:

Bradley, Timothy J. *Animal Architects* Huntington Beach, CA: Teacher Created Materials, 2012.
This book gives children a look at many amazing animal architects and how and why they build their homes.

Wilkes, Angela. *Animal Homes.*
New York, NY: Kingfisher, 2007.
This book introduces children to a number of animal's homes. Children will learn how to construct their own animal homes, including a nest and even a hamster playpen!

Perkins, Wendy. *Animals Building Homes.*
North Mankato, MN: Capstone Press, 2004.
This book explains the varied ways in which animals, such as beavers, termites, and hummingbirds, build their homes.

Websites:

http://newswatch.nationalgeographic.com/2014/01/27/5-animals-that-are-awesome-architects/
National Geographic provides more information about five awesome animal architects, including beavers, termites, and weaver birds.

www.pbs.org/wnet/nature/category/episodes/by-animal/beaver/
This website from PBS provides everything you need to know about beavers, including fact sheets and videos highlighting the benefits of beavers and how they build their homes.

www.kidport.com/reflib/science/animalhomes/animalhomes.htm
Discover the different kinds of homes animal's live in, from holes in the ground, to caves, nests, and trees.

Index